Learning English 3

Modern Course

Gym

Grammatisches Beiheft

Herausgegeben von Peter Pasch

Ernst Klett Stuttgart

Inhalt

			§§	Seite
Unit 1	Step 1:	Die Verlaufsform des Präsens mit einer Zeitangabe der Zukunft	1	4
	Step 2:	*Some* und *any* und ihre Zusammensetzungen	2	4
Unit 2	Step 5:	Der s-Genitiv ohne nachfolgendes Substantiv	3	5
		Adjektivische und substantivische Possessivpronomen	4	5
	Step 6:	Die Verlaufsform des Perfekt	5	6
		Zeitangaben mit *since* und *for*	6	6
	Step 7:	*What things? / Which of them?*	7	7
Unit 3	Step 9:	Das Plusquamperfekt	8	7
	Step 10:	Konjunktionen in Nebensätzen	9	8
Unit 4	Step 13—15:	Aktiv und Passiv	10	9
		Das Passiv: Formen und Gebrauch	11	9
	Step 16:	Das Passiv von *give, bring* usw.	12	10
		Das Reflexivpronomen zur Hervorhebung	13	10
Unit 5	Step 17:	*Can / be able to* zum Ausdruck einer Fähigkeit	14	11
		Must / have to zum Ausdruck einer Notwendigkeit	15	11
		Shall I? / Shall we?	16	12
		Should	17	12
	Step 18:	*May / be allowed to* zum Ausdruck einer Erlaubnis	18	12
		Once / twice / three times	19	13
		Die Steigerung von Adverbien	20	13
	Step 21:	Die Stellung unbestimmter Zeitadverbien	21	14
Unit 6	Step 22:	Relativsätze	22	14
	Step 23:	Nachstellung von Präpositionen in Relativsätzen	23	15
		Das Possessivpronomen mit *own*	24	15
Unit 7	Step 25:	Die indirekte Rede	25	16
	Step 26:	Der Imperativ in der indirekten Rede	26	17
Unit 8	Step 29:	Infinitivsätze mit *for*	27	17
	Step 30:	Das Stützwort *one / ones*	28	18

		§§	Seite
Übersichten	Unregelmäßige Plurale	29	18
	Nationalitätsbezeichnungen	30	19
Sprechabsichten	1. Begrüßung und Höflichkeitsformeln		20
	2. Wünsche, Bitten, Auskunft		20
	3. Anweisungen, Verbote		21
	4. Vorliebe, Abneigung, Gleichgültigkeit		22
	5. Pläne		22
	6. Zustimmung und Ablehnung		23
	7. Überraschung, Freude, Enttäuschung, Ärger, Bedauern		23
	8. Möglichkeit, Wahrscheinlichkeit, Sicherheit		24
	9. Begründungen		24
Alphabetisches Verzeichnis grammatischer Ausdrücke			25

Unit 1

Step 1

Die Verlaufsform des Präsens mit einer Zeitangabe der Zukunft § 1
(The Present Continuous with an Adverbial of future time)

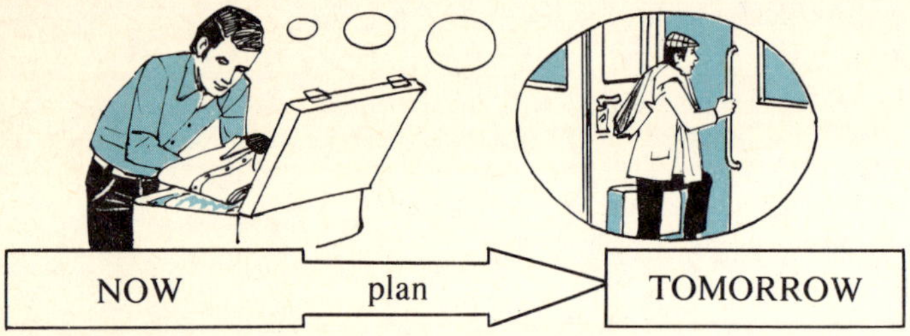

Mr Brown is packing his suitcase. He **is leaving** for his holidays **tomorrow.**

Um auszudrücken, daß etwas beabsichtigt, geplant oder vereinbart ist, kann die Verlaufsform des Präsens verwendet werden. Um Verwechslungen mit gegenwärtigen Handlungen auszuschließen, wird meist eine Zeitbestimmung der Zukunft benutzt. Diese ist jedoch nicht notwendig, wenn durch den Sinnzusammenhang klar ist, daß es sich um etwas Zukünftiges handelt.

Beachte: Auch das Futur mit *going to* kann einen Plan ausdrücken: *I'm going to buy a moped when I've got enough money.*

"I'**m leaving**	for my holidays	**tomorrow at 7 a.m.**"
"So you'**re** not **coming**	to our party	**tonight**? –
Are your sisters **coming**?"		
"No, they aren't. Sue'**s taking**	my parents to Bath	**at 8 p.m.,**
and Sandra'**s baby-sitting**	at the Smiths'	**from 7 to 10 p.m.**
Are your parents **staying**	in the house	**tonight**?"
"Oh, no. They'**re visiting**	London	**this week-end.**
They'**re leaving**	from the main station	**at 2 o'clock.**"

Step 2

"Some" und "any" und ihre Zusammensetzungen *(Some* and *any* and their Compounds) § 2

"Have we got	**any** bacon?		–	I think there's	**some**	in the cupboard."
"No, we haven't got	**any,**		–	and we need	**some** eggs,	too."
"Haven't we got	**anything**	for breakfast?	–	There must be	**something**	in the kitchen."
"No, we haven't got	**anything**	to eat in the house.	–	Perhaps we can get	**something**	from the Smiths."
"There isn't	**anyone (-body)**	in the garden."	–	"But I saw	**someone (-body)**	there a minute ago."
"Is there	**anyone (-body)**	in the house?"	–	"Yes, I can see	**someone (-body)**	through the window."
"I can't see my glasses	**anywhere.**"		–	"I think they're	**somewhere**	in the bedroom."
"No, they aren't. Are they	**anywhere**	in the bathroom?"	–	"Well, they must be	**somewhere.**"	

In Fragen und verneinten Sätzen stehen meist *any* und seine Zusammensetzungen, in bejahten Sätzen dagegen meist *some* und seine Zusammensetzungen.
Beachte: Auch *every* und *no* haben Zusammensetzungen:

everything alles	**everyone/everybody** jeder	**everywhere** überall
nothing ['nʌθiŋ] nichts	**no one/nobody** niemand	**nowhere** nirgends

Unit 2

Step 5

Der s-Genitiv ohne nachfolgendes Substantiv (The s-Genitive without a following Noun) §3

	"Whose **bike** is this?"	–	"It's	**Bob's.**"	„Es gehört Bob."
	"Are these Maggie's **shoes**?"	–	"No, they're	**Jane's.**"	„Nein, sie gehören Jane."
	"Look at that new **house**!"	–	"It's	**the Bartons'.**"	„Es gehört Bartons."

Der Besitzer einer Sache wird durch den s-Genitiv bezeichnet.
Das Substantiv nach dem s-Genitiv wird gewöhnlich weggelassen, wenn es kurz vorher genannt wurde.

Adjektivische und substantivische Possessivpronomen (Possessive Adjectives and Pronouns) §4

Possessive Adjectives + Nouns			**Possessive Pronouns**			
	"Isn't that Ist das nicht	**my** glass?" mein Glas?	–	"No, it's Nein, es ist	**mine.**" meins.	
	"This must be Das muß	**your** coat." Ihr Mantel sein.	–	"And this must be Und das muß	**yours.**" Ihrer	 sein.
	"Look, Tom has forgotten Schau mal, Tom hat	**his** books!" seine Bücher vergessen.	–	"Oh, no. They aren't Oh, nein. Das sind nicht	**his.**" seine.	
	"Aunt Jane was here." — "Is that Ist das	**her** umbrella?" ihr Schirm?	–	"No, Nein,	**hers** ihrer	isn't blue." ist nicht blau.
	"Here's Hier ist	**our** address." unsere Adresse.	–	"And here's Und hier ist	**ours.**" unsere.	
	"That's the Browns' house." — "Is this Ist das	**their** car?" ihr Wagen?	–	"No, Nein,	**theirs** ihrer	is bigger." ist größer.

Der Besitzer einer Sache kann auch durch ein Possessivpronomen bezeichnet werden.
Wenn ein Substantiv folgt, steht das *adjektivische* Possessivpronomen *(possessive adjective).*
Wird das Substantiv weggelassen, weil es bereits erwähnt wurde, so steht das *substantivische* Possessivpronomen *(possessive pronoun).*

Step 6

Die Verlaufsform des Perfekt (The Present Perfect Continuous) **§ 5**

"Waiter,	**I've been waiting** Ich warte (schon)	for my steak **since one o'clock.** I can't wait any longer." seit ein Uhr auf mein Steak.
"Look at these boys.	They've **been playing** Sie spielen (schon)	rugby **for two hours.** And they don't seem to be tired yet." seit zwei Stunden Rugby.
"It's half past five.	Chris **has been writing** Chris schreibt (schon)	letters **since lunch-time.** Hasn't he finished yet?" seit dem Mittagessen Briefe.
	"It's **been raining** Es regnet schon	**the whole week.** I hope the weather will change soon." die ganze Woche.

Das *Present Perfect Continuous* wird gebildet aus *have been* / *has been* und der *ing*-Form des Verbs.
Es bezeichnet einen Vorgang, der schon in der Vergangenheit anfing und noch nicht zu Ende ist (oder eben erst zu Ende ging).
Die Dauer des Vorgangs wird oft durch eine Zeitbestimmung mit *since* oder *for* angegeben.
Im Deutschen wird das Präsens benutzt, doch wird die Dauer des Geschehens häufig durch „schon" unterstrichen.

Zeitangaben mit "since" und "for" (Adverbials of time with *since* and *for*) **§ 6**

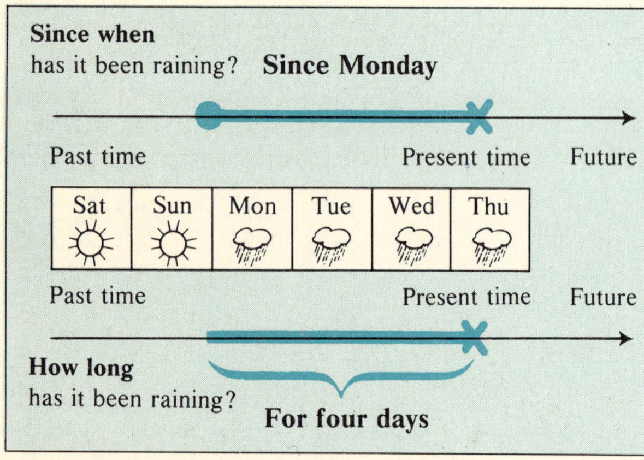

Since	half past two this morning Monday, February 28th October 1975 I arrived	**Seit**	halb drei heute morgen Montag, dem 28. Februar Oktober 1975 ich ankam
For	ten minutes two hours weeks a few months ten years a long time	**Seit**	zehn Minuten zwei Stunden Wochen ein paar Monaten zehn Jahren langem

Since rechnet von einem Zeitpunkt an (z. B. Uhrzeit, Tageszeit, Datum usw.).
For bezieht sich auf einen Zeitraum (z. B. Anzahl von Minuten, Stunden usw.).

Since when ...? fragt nach einem Zeitpunkt, *How long ... ?* nach einem Zeitraum.
Beachte: Auch Ausdrücke wie *the whole week* (die ganze Woche), *all day* (den ganzen Tag) usw. beziehen sich auf einen Zeitraum, der, wenn er bis zur Gegenwart reicht, das *Present Perfect Continuous* erfordert.

Step 7

What things?/Which of them? §7

What things **Which** of them	can you see on the table? can you eat?	Was für Dinge . . .? Welche (davon) . . .?
What animals **Which** of them	can you see here? eat grass?	Was für Tiere . . .? Welche (davon) . . .?
What instruments **Which** of them	are there in the shop-window? can *you* play?	Was für Instrumente . . .? Welche (davon) . . .?

What fragt nach Sachen allgemein.
Which fragt nach Sachen aus einer begrenzten Anzahl.

Unit 3 Step 9

Das Plusquamperfekt (The Past Perfect) §8

First we visited the UN Building. After that we walked to Central Park.	After we	**had visited**	the UN Building,	we	walked	to Central Park.
Julie went out. Five minutes later Martin phoned.	Julie	**had gone out,**		when Martin	phoned.	
Peggy looked at all the clothes. At last she bought a blue pullover.	When Peggy	**had looked**	at all the clothes,	she	bought	a blue pullover.
The rain stopped. Later they came out of the disco.	The rain	**had stopped**	when they		came	out of the disco.

Das *Past Perfect* wird mit *had* und dem Partizip Perfekt *(past participle)* gebildet.
Wenn zwei Vorgänge der Vergangenheit in Beziehung zueinander gebracht werden sollen, so wird der Vorgang, der weiter zurückliegt, durch das *Past Perfect* ausgedrückt.
Beachte: Geschehen beide Vorgänge zum gleichen Zeitpunkt, so steht das *Past Tense.*

Julie **went out** when Martin **phoned.**
The rain **stopped** when they **came out** of the disco.

Step 10

Konjunktionen in Nebensätzen §9
(Conjunctions in Subordinate Clauses)

Main Clause (Hauptsatz)	**Subordinate Clause** (Nebensatz)		
Two cowboys rode into town.			
They stopped	**when**	they reached the saloon.	... **als** sie zum Saloon kamen.
They had three glasses of whisky	**before**	they ordered a meal.	... **bevor** sie etwas zu essen bestellten.
They drank a lot of beer	**while**	they were eating.	... **während** sie aßen.
They did not get up	**until**	they had eaten everything.	... **bis** sie alles aufgegessen hatten.
They gave their horses some food	**after**	they had had another drink.	... **nachdem** sie noch etwas getrunken hatten.
Three hours had passed	**since**	they had arrived.	... **seit** sie angekommen waren.
They did not ride home,	**although**	it was very late.	... **obwohl** es sehr spät war.
They went back to the saloon	**because**	they wanted to play cards.	... **weil** sie Karten spielen wollten.
	As	they were still thirsty,	**Da** sie immer noch Durst hatten ...
they had another whisky.			
They sat down in the corner	**so that**	they could see everybody.	... **damit** sie jeden sehen konnten.
Suddenly one of them shouted:			
"I'll throw that bottle at you	**if**	you don't give me the money!"	... **wenn** du mir nicht das Geld gibst.
"I'll throw you out	**unless**	you put that bottle down," said the barman.	... **wenn** du **nicht** die Flasche wegstellst.

Die Konjunktionen im blauen Feld leiten Nebensätze ein.
In den meisten Fällen kann der Nebensatz auch vor dem Hauptsatz stehen.

Beachte: 1. Nebensätze, die mit *as* („da", „weil") eingeleitet werden, stehen meistens vor dem Hauptsatz. Nebensätze mit *because* werden gewöhnlich nachgestellt.

2. Jim went to Florida **in order to** get well again.
Jim ging nach Florida, **um** wieder gesund **zu** werden.

In order to leitet immer einen Infinitivsatz ein.

Unit 4

Step 13 – 15

Aktiv und Passiv (Active and Passive Voice) **§ 10**

	**Active Voice** **The policeman** *arrested* the thief.		**Passive Voice** **The thief** *was arrested* (by the policeman).

Im Englischen wie im Deutschen kann die gleiche Handlung manchmal auf zwei verschiedene Arten ausgedrückt werden.
Im oben dargestellten Fall sind zwei Personen beteiligt:

1. Beim *Aktiv* ist der Handelnde das grammatische Subjekt des Satzes.
2. Beim *Passiv* ist der von der Handlung betroffene das grammatische Subjekt des Satzes. Er steht im Vordergrund der Betrachtung.

Das Passiv: Formen und Gebrauch (The Passive Voice: Forms and Usage) **§ 11**

a)	Lunch	**is served**	at 12 o'clock.		Das Mittagessen wird um 12 Uhr serviert.
	It	**is served**		**by** French waiters.	Es wird von französischen Kellnern serviert.
	The beds	**are made**	every morning.		Die Betten werden jeden Morgen gemacht.
	They	**are made**		**by** the hotel girls.	Sie werden von den Zimmermädchen gemacht.
b)	The house	**was built**	in 1950.		Das Haus wurde 1950 gebaut.
	It	**was built**		**by** Brown & Co.	Es wurde von Brown & Co. gebaut.
	New windows	**were put in**	two years ago.		Neue Fenster wurden vor zwei Jahren eingebaut.
	They	**were put in**		**by** Smith & Co.	Sie wurden von Smith & Co. eingebaut.
c)	Our bank	**has been robbed.**			Unsere Bank ist ausgeraubt worden.
	A clerk	**has been injured**		**by** the robbers.	... ist von den Banditen verletzt worden.
	Several houses	**have been damaged**		**by** the wind.	... sind durch den Wind beschädigt worden.
	A lot of windows	**have been broken.**			Viele Scheiben sind zerbrochen worden.
d)	The dustbin	**must be emptied.**			Der Mülleimer muß geleert werden.
	The street	**must be swept.**			Die Straße muß gekehrt werden.
	Rubbish	**mustn't be thrown**	into ponds.		Abfall darf nicht in Teiche geworfen werden.
	Dogs	**mustn't be taken**	into the shop.		Hunde dürfen nicht mit ... genommen werden.

1. Das Passiv wird gebildet aus einer Form von *to be* und dem Partizip Perfekt *(past participle).*
   Die Formen von *to be* lauten
   a) im Präsens *am / is / are*
   b) im Präteritum *was / were*
   c) im Perfekt *has been / have been*
   d) im Infinitiv *be* (unverändert).
2. Das Passiv wird vor allem dann verwendet, wenn man den Handelnden nicht nennen kann oder will, weil er nicht bekannt oder nicht wichtig ist.
   Will man den Handelnden ausdrücklich nennen, so wird er durch *by* eingeführt.

Step 16

Das Passiv von "give", "bring" usw. (The Passive Voice of *give, bring,* etc.) § 12

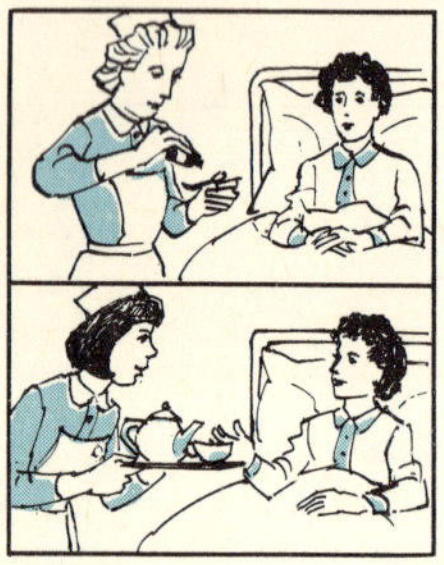

Active Voice:

1. The nurse gave **the patient** some medicine.

2. Later another nurse brought **her** some tea.

Passive Voice:

The patient was given some medicine.

Later **she** was brought some tea.

Verben wie *give* und *bring* können im Aktiv zwei Objekte haben: ein indirektes Objekt, meist eine Person (vgl. *the patient, her*) und ein direktes Objekt, meist eine Sache (vgl. *some medicine, some tea*).

Im Passiv kann das indirekte Objekt des Aktivsatzes zum Subjekt werden (vgl. *the patient, she*). Dies ist jedoch nur bei einer begrenzten Anzahl von Verben möglich.

Weitere Beispiele:

When Judy was in hospital,	**she**	**was sent**	a lot of flowers.	... bekam sie viele Blumen.
Mr Brown has sold his old Morris.	**He**	**was paid**	£200 for it.	Er bekam £200 dafür.
In Petticoat Lane	**I**	**was sold**	a guitar for £5.	... bekam ich eine Gitarre für £5.
The old lady was glad when	**she**	**was offered**	a seat.	... als ihr jemand einen Platz anbot.
The sightseeing tour was interesting.	**We**	**were shown**	the whole castle.	Man zeigte uns das ganze Schloß.
The children were hungry.	**They**	**were given**	some sandwiches.	Sie bekamen ein paar Sandwiches.
When the guests arrived	**they**	**were brought**	some drinks.	... wurden ihnen Getränke gebracht.
Were you surprised when	**you**	**were told**	what had happened?	... als Sie erfuhren, was passiert war?

Das Reflexivpronomen zur Hervorhebung (The Reflexive Pronoun: Emphatic Usage) § 13

"Can I wash your car?" — "No, thank you,	**I**	'm going to do it	**myself.**"
"Could you ring up Mr Brown for me?" — "Why don't	**you**	ring him up	**yourself?**"
"Dad needs some help.	**He**	can't do all the work	**himself.**"
"Miss Croft doesn't need a mechanic.	**She**	can repair her car	**herself.**"
"We can put up the wallpaper for you." — "No, thanks,	**we**	'd like to do it	**ourselves.**"
"Can you help us with the table?" — "No,	**you**	can carry it	**yourselves.**"
"Tom and Mary didn't leave us any of the sweets.	**They**	ate them all	**themselves.**"

Das Reflexivpronomen kann zur Hervorhebung eines Personalpronomens oder einer Person dienen. Es steht dann meist am Ende des Satzes und entspricht dem deutschen *selbst / allein.*

Beachte: 1. Die Reflexivpronomen haben im Singular die Endung *-self* und im Plural die Endung *-selves.*
2. *you ... yourself* richtet sich an eine einzige Person: *du ... selbst / Sie* (Singular) *... selbst.*
you ... yourselves richtet sich an mehrere Personen: *ihr ... selbst / Sie* (Plural) *... selbst.*

Unit 5 Step 17

"Can"/"be able to" zum Ausdruck einer Fähigkeit **§ 14**
(*can / be able to* to express ability)

1. a)		**"Can**	Mrs Cook walk again?"			
	("**Is** Mrs Cook	**able to**	walk again?")			
	– "She	**can**	walk a few steps,	but she	**can't**	go out yet.
	("She	**'s able to**	walk a few steps,	but she	**isn't able to**	go out yet.)
b)	Yesterday she	**was able to**	sit in the garden,	but she	**couldn't**	walk around."
				(but she	**wasn't able to**	walk around.")
2.	– "**Has** she	**been able to**	get a home help?" – "She tried to,	but they	**haven't been able to**	send anyone yet."
	– "**Will** she	**be able to**	go out again soon?"			
	– "She	**'ll be able to**	go shopping in a month,	but she	**won't be able to**	carry heavy bags."

1. a) Eine Fähigkeit wird im Präsens sehr häufig durch *can* ausgedrückt. Daneben werden auch Formen von *to be able to* verwendet.
   b) Zu *can* gibt es die Past-Tense-Form *could (konnte).* Im Sinne einer vorübergehenden Fähigkeit *(schaffte es gerade, war fähig, war in der Lage zu ...)* tritt jedoch in bejahten Sätzen die entsprechende Form von *to be able to* ein.
2. Für *Present Perfect, Past Perfect* und *Future* treten stets die entsprechenden Formen des Ersatzverbs *to be able to* ein.

"Must"/"have to" zum Ausdruck einer Notwendigkeit **§ 15**
(*must / have to* to express necessity)

1.	*Sue:*	**"Must**	you really go home already?"	*Tina:* "Well, I	**needn't**	go home, yet,
				I	**don't have to**	be home before eleven."
	Steve: "But I	**must**	leave now,			
	I	**have to**	be home by 10 o'clock."			
	Sue: "When **does** John	**have to**	be home?" *Steve:* "At half past ten."			
2.	"Why **did** the Macmillans	**have to**	move?"			
	– "Because Mr Macmillan	**had to**	take a job in Aberdeen." –	"At least they	**didn't have to**	leave Scotland."
	– "They	**'ve had to**	leave their mother here." –	"But they	**haven't had to**	send her to a home."
	– "Perhaps they	**'ll have to**	one day.	Of course they hope she	**won't have to**	leave her house until she dies."

1. Dem deutschen *müssen* zum Ausdruck einer Notwendigkeit entspricht im Präsens *must* oder eine Form von *to have to.*
   Dem deutschen *nicht müssen, nicht brauchen* entspricht im Präsens *needn't* oder *doesn't / don't have to.*
   Bei *must* geht das „muß" gewöhnlich vom Sprecher aus, während es bei *have to* von einer dritten Person ausgeht oder allgemeiner Art ist.
2. Für *Past Tense, Present Perfect, Past Perfect* und *Future* treten stets die entsprechenden Formen des Ersatzverbs *to have to* ein.

Beachte: Fragen mit **to have to** werden in *Present* und *Past Tense* mit der *do*-Umschreibung gebildet.

Shall I?/Shall we? § 16

"It's hot in here.	**Shall**	**I**	open the window?" — "Yes, all right."	Soll ich ...?
"Here's the new table. Where	**shall**	**we**	put it?" — "Leave it in the hall, please."	... sollen wir ...?
"The weather's fine.	**Shall**	**we**	go swimming?" — "Good idea."	Sollen wir ... ?/Wollen wir ...?

Shall fragt wie das deutsche *sollen* nach einem Wunsch oder drückt einen Vorschlag aus.

Should § 17

"You	**should**	go to the doctor's."	Du solltest ...
"I know I	**should,**	but I haven't got time."	... daß ich (das tun) sollte, ...
"We	**should**	visit grandmother more often."	Wir sollten ...
"John	**shouldn't**	smoke so much."	John sollte nicht ...

Should drückt, wie das deutsche *sollte*, einen Rat, eine Ermahnung oder eine Verpflichtung aus.

Step 18

"May"/"be allowed to" zum Ausdruck einer Erlaubnis § 18
(*May / be allowed to* to express permission)

1.		"**May**	I smoke?"			
	— "Yes, you	**may,**	if you're sixteen,	but you	**mustn't**	smoke in the dormitory."
		"**May**	we go to a party tonight?"			
	— "Yes, you	**may,**		but you	**mustn't**	stay longer than 10 o'clock."
	John	**is allowed**	to smoke,	but he	**isn't allowed to**	smoke in the dormitory.
	"**Are** you	**allowed**	to go to parties, Mary?"			
	— "Yes, I	**am,**		but I	**'m not allowed to**	stay longer than ten."
2.	Jim and Sue	**were allowed to**	visit their uncle last week-end,	but they	**weren't allowed to**	spend the night there.
	"Was Jim	**allowed to**	go to the cinema last night?" —	"No, he	**wasn't.**"	
	Jane	**has been allowed to**	go out since she left school,	but she	**hasn't been allowed to**	stay away from home.
	Girls	**have been allowed to**	wear jeans at our school for years,	but they	**haven't been allowed to**	wear shorts.
	Peggy	**will be allowed to**	invite some friends on her birthday,	but she	**won't be allowed to**	invite more than six.
	"Will you	**be allowed to**	have a big birthday party, Peggy?" —	"No, I	**won't.**"	

1. Im Präsens kann eine Erlaubnis durch *may* oder eine Form von *to be allowed to* ausgedrückt werden. (Deutsch: *dürfen*)
   Ein Verbot kann durch *mustn't* oder eine verneinte Form von *to be allowed to* ausgedrückt werden. (Deutsch: *nicht dürfen*)
   May kommt hauptsächlich in Fragen und bejahenden Antworten vor.
2. Für *Past Tense, Present Perfect, Past Perfect* und *Future* werden die entsprechenden Formen des Ersatzverbs *to be allowed to* verwendet.

Once/twice/three times § 19

Mrs Black only goes shopping on Mondays. She goes shopping	**once**	**a** week.	... einmal **pro** Woche ...
Mrs Roberts does the washing-up after lunch and after supper. She does it	**twice**	**a** day.	... zweimal **am** Tag ...
Mrs Cook sees three films a month. She goes to the cinema	**three times**	**a** month.	... dreimal **im** Monat ...
Mrs Wood cleans the windows in winter, spring, summer and autumn. She cleans them	**four times**	**a** year.	... viermal **im** Jahr ...

Nach dem Muster von *three times* und *four times* werden auch die anderen Wiederholungszahlen gebildet, z. B. *a hundred and twelve times, two thousand times.*

Die Steigerung von Adverbien (The Comparison of Adverbs) § 20

	Sue can see the moon	**clearly**.	Jim can run	**fast**.	
	Peter can see it	**more clearly**.	Tom can run	**faster**.	
	Mr Brown can see it	**most clearly** of all.	Peter can run	**fastest** of all.	
	Mr Sharp drives	**dangerously**.	Mr Clark can sing	**well**.	
	Miss Price drives	**more dangerously**.	Mary can sing	**better**.	
	Mr Smith drives	**most dangerously** of all.	Mrs Hall can sing	**best** of all.	

Adverbien mit der Endung *-ly* bilden den Komparativ mit *more* und den Superlativ mit *most.*
Einsilbige Adverbien wie *fast* werden mit *-er / -est* gesteigert.

Beachte: 1. Die Steigerungsformen von *well* lauten *better, best.*
2. *Most* kann auch die Bedeutung „sehr, äußerst, höchst" haben,
z. B. *You'll* **most** *probably go to my school.* („... höchstwahrscheinlich ...")

Step 21

Die Stellung unbestimmter Zeitadverbien (The Position of Adverbs of Indefinite Time) **§ 21**

The children are disappointed.	They have	**not**	been	allowed to go swimming today.	Sie haben heute nicht schwimmen gehen dürfen.
We are moving next month.	But we have	**not**	been	able to find a new flat **yet.**	Wir haben noch keine neue Wohnung finden können.
Mr Brown often goes to Paris.	But he has	**not yet**	been	able to visit the South of France.	Es war ihm noch nicht möglich, Südfrankreich zu besuchen.
He doesn't know much about cars.	He has	**often**	had	to take his car to the garage.	Er hat seinen Wagen schon oft zur Werkstatt bringen müssen.
Tim has always got a lot of work.	He has	**sometimes**	had	to work on Sundays.	Er hat (schon) ein paarmal sonntags arbeiten müssen.
Mrs Wood is seriously ill.	She will	**never**	be	allowed to smoke again.	Sie wird nie mehr rauchen dürfen.
My parents won't buy me a bike.	I will	**always**	have	to walk to school.	Ich werde immer zu Fuß zur Schule gehen müssen.

Wie das Adverb der Verneinung *not* stehen die unbestimmten Zeitadverbien bei zusammengesetzten Zeiten unmittelbar nach dem ersten Hilfsverb.
Beachte: *Yet* steht gewöhnlich am Ende des Satzes, kann aber auch unmittelbar hinter *not* stehen.

Unit 6

Step 22

Relativsätze (Relative Clauses) **§ 22**

	The man	**who (that)**	saved the crew	was a Moslem.	Der Mann, der die Mannschaft rettete, ...
	The people	**who (that)**	have moved into that house	come from India.	Die Leute, die in das Haus dort eingezogen sind, ...
	The black car	**which (that)**	is parked over there	is Mr Brown's.	Der schwarze Wagen, der dort drüben parkt, ...
	The boat	**which (that)**	was lying on the beach	belonged to Alan.	Das Boot, das am Strand lag, ...

Das Relativpronomen *who* bezieht sich auf Personen. *Which* bezieht sich auf Sachen (und auch auf abstrakte Begriffe und Tiere). *That* kann sich sowohl auf Personen als auch auf Sachen beziehen.
Beachte: *The scarf (which) Judy found in the street belonged to Mrs Sharp.* Das Relativpronomen kann weggelassen werden, wenn es Objekt des Relativsatzes ist, und wenn der Relativsatz zum Verständnis des Hauptsatzes notwendig ist. Relativsätze mit fehlenden Relativpronomen nennt man *contact clauses.* (Siehe Grammatisches Beiheft 2, § 44)

Step 23

Nachstellung von Präpositionen in Relativsätzen §23
(End-Position of Prepositions in Relative Clauses)

A vacuum cleaner is a machine	**with**	**which**	we clean carpets.			... eine Maschine, **mit der** wir Teppiche reinigen.
A vacuum cleaner is a machine		**which**	we clean carpets	**with.**		
A vacuum cleaner is a machine		**that**	we clean carpets	**with.**		
A vacuum cleaner is a machine			we clean carpets	**with.**		
Is this the book	**for**	**which**	you are looking?			... das Buch, **nach dem** du suchst?
Is this the book		**which**	you are looking	**for**?		
Is this the book		**that**	you are looking	**for**?		
Is this the book			you are looking	**for**?		
Do you know the man		**who**	I was talking	**to**	at the post office?	... der Mann, **mit dem** ich auf dem Postamt sprach?
Do you know the man		**that**	I was talking	**to**	at the post office?	
Do you know the man			I was talking	**to**	at the post office?	
Yesterday I saw the interviewer		**who**	you told me	**about.**		... der Interviewer, **von dem** du mir erzählt hast.
Yesterday I saw the interviewer		**that**	you told me	**about.**		
Yesterday I saw the interviewer			you told me	**about.**		

Bei *which* steht die Präposition gelegentlich vor dem Relativpronomen, vor allem in der Schriftsprache.
In der Umgangssprache wird sie jedoch fast immer hinter das Verb und sein Objekt gestellt.
Bei *who* und *that*, oder wenn das Relativpronomen entfällt (*contact clauses*), wird die Präposition immer nachgestellt.

Das Possessivpronomen mit "own" (The Possessive Adjective with *own*) §24

"Margaret's got	**her own**	car now.	She's happy, because she's got	a car **of her own.**"
	ihren eigenen	Wagen		einen eigenen Wagen
"Uncle Fred's got	**his own**	umbrella."	—"Then he doesn't need ours, if he's got	an umbrella **of his own.**"
	seinen eigenen	Schirm		einen eigenen Schirm
"I've got	**my own**	records.	I don't need hers, because I've got more than	20 records **of my own.**"
	meine eigenen	Schallplatten		20 eigene Schallplatten
"Bob and Joe have got	**their own**	footballs.	They want to play with ours! But they've got	two balls **of their own.**"
	ihre eigenen	Fußbälle		zwei eigene Bälle

Own verstärkt das adjektivische Possessivpronomen.
Es sind zwei Stellungen möglich:
1. Das Possessivpronomen und *own* stehen vor dem Substantiv (wie im Deutschen).
2. Wenn vor dem Substantiv der unbestimmte Artikel oder ein Zahlwort steht, so wird *own* in der Form *of my own* (*of your own*, etc.) dem Substantiv nachgestellt.

Beachte: Im Gegensatz zum deutschen Adjektiv *eigen* steht *own* nie unmittelbar nach dem unbestimmten Artikel oder einem Zahlwort: Vor *own* steht immer ein Possessivpronomen.

Unit 7

Step 25

Die indirekte Rede §25
(Reported Speech)

Direct Speech			Reported Speech *(Main Clause in the Past Tense)*		
1. *Mrs Barratt:*			1. Mrs. Barratt *said* (that)		
"Our toaster	**is**	out of order, and	their toaster	**was**	out of order,
the electric stove	**doesn't work.**"		and (that) the electric stove	**didn't work.**	
2. *Mr Barratt:*			2. Mr Barratt *remarked* (that)		
"Perhaps a fuse	**has blown.**		perhaps a fuse	**had blown.**	
	Have you **checked**	the fuses?"	He *asked* his wife if she	**had checked**	the fuses.
Mrs Barratt: "Yes, I	**have.**	They're O.K."	She *replied* (that) she	**had,**	they were O.K.
3. *Mrs Barratt:* "I	**telephoned**	the repairs department this morning."	3. Then she *told* him (that) she	**had telephoned**	the repairs department that morning.
Mr Barratt: "What	**did** they **say**?"		He *wanted to know* what they	**had said.**	
4. *Mrs Barratt:* "They	**'ll send**	someone tomorrow."	4. She *said* (that) they	**would send**	someone the next day.
Mr Barratt: "So you	**won't be able to**	cook until then."	Mr Barratt *remarked* (that) she	**wouldn't be able to**	cook until then.

Die indirekte Rede ist die indirekte (d. h. nicht wörtliche) Wiedergabe einer Aussage, einer Frage, eines Gedankens usw. Sie wird meist eingeleitet durch einen Satz, der ein Verb wie *say, tell, ask, answer* usw. enthält (Einleitungssatz). Steht dieser Einleitungssatz im *Past Tense,* so ergeben sich bei der Wiedergabe der Rede folgende Zeitverschiebungen:

Direkte Rede		Indirekte Rede
1. **Present Tense**	→	**Past Tense**
2. **Present Perfect**	→	**Past Perfect**
3. **Past Tense**	→	**Past Perfect**
4. **will + Infinitive**	→	**would + Infinitive**

Beachte: 1. Die Konjunktion *that* in der indirekten Rede kann weggelassen werden.
2. Indirekte Fragen beginnen, wenn kein Fragewort vorhanden ist, mit *if* oder *whether* (Deutsch: *ob*).
3. Bei der Umwandlung von der direkten zur indirekten Rede verändern sich meist auch die Zeitangaben,
z. B. *this morning* (*week*, etc.) → *that morning* (*week*, etc.)
today → *that day*
yesterday → *the day before*
tomorrow → *the next day*

Step 26

Der Imperativ in der indirekten Rede **§ 26**
(Indirect Commands)

Imperatives		Indirect Commands				
Stewardess:		The stewardess				
"Stop	smoking, please."	**asked**	the passengers		**to stop**	smoking.
"Fasten	your seat-belts."	She **asked**	them		**to fasten**	their seat-belts.
"Put	your bags under your seats."	She **told**	them		**to put**	their bags under their seats.
"Don't stand up	during the take-off."	She **warned**	them	**not**	**to stand up**	during the take-off.

Ein Imperativ wird in der indirekten Rede durch einen Infinitiv mit **to** wiedergegeben.
Beachte: In Verbindung mit indirekten Befehlen entspricht *asked* dem deutschen „bat", *told* entspricht „wies an", *warned ... (not) to* entspricht „ermahnte ... (nicht) zu".

Unit 8

Step 29

Infinitivsätze mit "for" **§ 27**
(Infinitive clauses with *for*)

It is **not easy**	**for** pilots	**to fly**	in thunderstorms.	Es ist nicht leicht für Piloten, bei Gewitter zu fliegen.
Jane hopes it will be **possible**	**for** her	**to study**	music.	... daß sie die Möglichkeit haben wird, Musik zu studieren.
It has been **wonderful**	**for** us	**to fly**	in a jumbo jet.	Wir fanden es wundervoll, in einem Jumbojet zu fliegen.
It was **necessary**	**for** the astronauts	**to wear**	special clothes.	Es war notwendig, daß die Astronauten Spezialkleidung trugen.
It is **too cold**	**for** the children	**to swim**	today.	Für die Kinder ist es heute zum Schwimmen zu kalt.
The suitcases are **too heavy**	**for** you	**to carry**.		Die Koffer sind zu schwer für dich.

Viele Adjektive können Infinitivsätze mit *for* und eigenem Sinnsubjekt (*the pilots, the astronauts,* etc.) nach sich ziehen. Das Deutsche muß zum Teil auf andere Konstruktionen ausweichen.

Step 30

Das Stützwort "one/ones" (The Prop Word *one / ones*) **§ 28**

Mary has got three **pullovers,** and	a blue **one** two white **ones.**		. . ., einen blauen und zwei weiße.
"Which **umbrella** do you want, or	the long **one** the short **one**?"		„. . ., den langen oder den kurzen?"
"Which of those **women** is your aunt?"	"The thin **one.**"		. . . „Die dünne."

Soll ein vorher genanntes Substantiv nicht wiederholt werden, so tritt hinter das Adjektiv an seine Stelle das Stützwort *one* (im Plural *ones*).

Beachte:

> "Which **umbrella** do you want, this **one** or that **one**?"
> "Which of those women is your aunt?" — "The **one** who is wearing glasses." (—"The **one** with the short hair." — "The **one** on the left", etc.)

One / ones kann ein Substantiv auch bei anderen Bestimmungen vertreten, z. B. nach *this, that,* vor einem Relativsatz oder bei einer adverbialen Bestimmung.

Übersichten

Unregelmäßige Plurale (Irregular Plurals) **§ 29**

1.	a man [æ] a woman ['wumən] a child [ai] a foot [u] a goose [u:] a tooth [u:] a mouse [au]	three men [e] five women ['wimin] four children [i] two feet [i:] ten geese [i:] 32 teeth [i:] three mice [ai]	Diese Wörter bilden den Plural nicht mit *-s*; statt dessen verändern sich die Vokale.
2.	a calf a wolf a loaf a knife his wife my life [f]	some calves three wolves four loaves five knives their wives our lives [vz]	Singular *-f(e)* [f] Plural *-ves* [vz]. Ebenso: a bookshelf, 2 bookshelves
3.	a fish a sheep	several fish a lot of sheep	Gleiche Form in Singular und Plural.
4.	a potat**o** a tomat**o** a Negr**o**	three potat**oes** ten tomat**oes** some Negr**oes**	Singular *-o*, Plural *-oes.*
5.	His furniture My hair The information This news	**is** old **is** wet. **is** interesting. **is** good.	Im Englischen immer Singular, im Deutschen meist Plural (*seine Möbel, meine Haare* usw.).
6.	The stairs The scales My shorts Her trousers His pyjamas Her glasses	**are** dangerous. **are** on the counter. **are** dirty. **are** too long. **are** on the bed. **are** broken.	Im Englischen immer Plural, im Deutschen meist Singular (*Die Treppe ist gefährlich*, etc.). **Beachte:** Nach Zahlwort oder unbest. Artikel: two **pairs of** shorts a **pair of** scales, etc.

Nationalitätsbezeichnungen (Nationality words) **§ 30**

Country	Adjective			Person	The People	Language(s)
Algeria	an	**Algerian**	town	an Algerian	the Algerians	Arabic
Australia	an	**Australian**	animal	an Australian	the Australians	English
Austria	an	**Austrian**	driver	an Austrian	the Austrians	German
Canada	a	**Canadian**	firm	a Canadian	the Canadians	English, French
England	an	**English**	book	an Englishman/woman	the English	English
France	a	**French**	stewardess	a Frenchman/woman	the French	French
Denmark	a	**Danish**	ship	a Dane	the Danes (the Danish)	Danish
Germany	a	**German**	teacher	a German	the Germans	German
Great Britain	a	**British**	airline	a Briton	the British	English
Holland (The Netherlands)	a	**Dutch**	trawler	a Dutchman/woman	the Dutch	Dutch
India	an	**Indian**	scarf	an Indian	the Indians	many languages
Ireland	an	**Irish**	folk song	an Irishman/woman	the Irish	English, Gaelic ['geilik] (Irish)
Italy	an	**Italian**	car	an Italian	the Italians	Italian
Mexico ['meksikəu]	a	**Mexican**	drink	a Mexican	the Mexicans	Spanish
Morocco	a	**Moroccan**	bag	a Moroccan	the Moroccans	Arabic
Pakistan [ˌpɑ:ki'stɑ:n]	a	**Pakistani**	doctor	a Pakistani	the Pakistanis	many languages
Poland	a	**Polish**	pilot	a Pole	the Poles (the Polish)	Polish
Russia ['rʌʃə] (The Soviet Union)	a	**Russian**	plane	a Russian	the Russians	Russian
Scotland	a	**Scottish**	island	a Scot, a Scotsman/woman	the Scots (the Scottish)	English
Spain	a	**Spanish**	dance	a Spaniard	the Spanish (the Spaniards)	Spanish
Switzerland	a	**Swiss**	watch	a Swiss	the Swiss	German, French, Italian
The United States of America	an	**American**	spaceship	an American	the Americans	English

1. Von Ländernamen abgeleitete Adjektive auf *-(i)an* dienen auch zur Bezeichnung einzelner Einwohner *(an Algerian, two Algerians)* oder des ganzen Volkes *(the Algerians)*. Der Plural wird mit *-s* gebildet.

2. Adjektive auf *-ch (French, Dutch)* und *-ish* dienen häufig auch zur Bezeichnung des ganzen Volkes, z. B.: *The French, the British* usw. (kein Plural *-s*!).
   Einzelne Einwohner haben in diesem Fall besondere Bezeichnungen, z. B.:
   a Frenchman (-woman), two Frenchmen (-women); a Briton, two Britons.

Beachte: Zur Bezeichnung der Nationalität kann man sowohl ein Substantiv als auch ein Adjektiv verwenden, z. B.:
His father is an Englishman oder *His father is English. — I'm a German* oder *I'm German.*

Sprechabsichten

Wenn man mit jemandem spricht, so verfolgt man eine bestimmte Absicht: Man möchte ihm z. B. Meinungen oder Empfindungen mitteilen oder ihn veranlassen, etwas zu tun.
In der folgenden Übersicht sind die häufigsten *Sprechabsichten* in 9 Abschnitten zusammengefaßt. Die Beispiele in den einzelnen Abschnitten zeigen, wie man eine Sprechabsicht mit dem Wortschatz und den Strukturen von *Learning English — Modern Course 1—3* auf recht unterschiedliche Weise ausdrücken kann. Die für eine Sprechabsicht typischen Ausdrücke sind durch **Fettdruck** hervorgehoben.

1. Begrüßung und Höflichkeitsformeln
(Greetings and Polite Expressions)

What can you say when you meet someone or say good-bye to someone?

Hello, John. Come in.
Hi, Barbara.
Good morning, Mr Johnson. This way please.
Good afternoon, Mrs Wilson.
Good evening, Miss Warner.
How do you do?

Nice to see you.
How are you? — Fine thanks./I feel awful.
What's the matter (with you)? — Nothing./Nothing much.
What's wrong with you? — I'm terrified. We've got an English test today.
How are you feeling now? — All right./O.K.
How's your mother? — She's feeling much better today.

'Bye, Helen.
Bye-bye, Anne.
See you later (tomorrow/at six o'clock).
Good-bye, Mr Black.
Good night, Mrs Green.

Give my love to Sally.
Give my regards to your father.

Have a nice time. — Thanks.
Good luck. — Thanks a lot.
All the best. — The same to you.
Have a good flight. — Thank you.
Happy birthday, Mr Parker. — Thank you very much.

2. Wünsche, Bitten, Auskunft
(Wishes, Requests, Asking for Information)

a) What can you say if you want something/if someone asks you for something?

A cup of tea, **please.** — **Here you are.**
Milk for Colin and lemonade for me, **please.** — **All right.**
Bring me a glass of milk, **please.** — **Sorry, we haven't got any.**
I want/I need a box of matches. — **O.K., that's** 4p.
I'd like a cup of coffee. — **Just a minute, I'll get you one.**
Have you got any new potatoes? — **Yes, certainly.**
Can/Could/Would you lend me your knife, **please?** — **Of course, here you are.**
May/Can/Could I use your biro? — **Sorry,** it doesn't work.
I like that pullover, **I'll have** that. — **Certainly,** madam/sir.
I wish we could go to Spain. — Well, why don't we?

b) What can you say if you want to offer someone something/if someone offers you something?

A cup of tea, Colin? — **Yes, please.**
Anything else? — **No, thank you.**
Let me help you. — **Thank you very much.**
Can I help you? — **Thanks a lot.**
What can I do for you? — A pound of butter, **please.**
Can I do anything for you? — **No, thank you,** I'm all right.
May I offer you a cigarette? — **No, thanks,** I don't smoke.
You need a new pen? **Take** this one. / **I'll get you** one. — **Many thanks.**
Can I give you a hand? — **Thanks, but** I can manage myself.
Shall I fetch some help? — **Yes,** and **please** be quick.
I'm going to get you a drink. — **Oh, that's awfully nice of you.**

c) What can you say if you need some information about place or time/if someone asks you about place or time?

Excuse me, officer, **where's** the nearest telephone box? — Just round the corner, sir/madam.
Can/Could you tell me the way to the station, **please?** — Turn right here. Then second on the left ...
How do I get to Trafalgar Square? — Take that bus over there.
Where's that train **going to?** — **To** Birmingham, Crewe and Manchester.
Can I go to Waterloo Station **by** Underground? — Yes, of course. It's only two stops.
Could you tell me if there's a post office near here? — **I'm afraid I don't know.**
Excuse me, where can I get a snack at the station? — Just inside the main entrance.

Excuse me, what time is it? — **It's exactly** 25 past seven.
When's the next bus **to** Wimbledon, **please?** — **In** ten minutes.
How long does it take to get there? — **About** twenty minutes.
Can you tell me when the Bristol train leaves? — **At** 10.47 a.m.

3. Anweisungen, Verbote, Erlaubnis
(Instructions, Prohibitions, Permission)

a) What can you say if you want someone to do something?

Wait for us, **please.**
Be quick.
You should stop smoking.
You must be more careful next time.
You've got flu'. **You'll have to** stay in bed.
Can/Could/Would you open the window, **please**?
Why don't you sit down?

b) What can you say if you don't want someone to do something?

Don't be late.
Don't move, **please.**
You're not going out in those jeans!
You shouldn't drink so much whisky.
You mustn't get up yet. You've still got a temperature.
You're not allowed to park your car here.
You can't wear that awful pullover at the party.

c) What can you say if you want permission to do something/if someone asks you for permission to do something?

May I watch the TV programme at 9 o'clock? — **Yes, you may./Yes, of course.**
Can I go swimming this afternoon? — **No, you can't.** It's too cold.
Could I go to the cinema then? — **All right. I don't mind.**
Are you **allowed to** smoke in a theatre? — No, you aren't. **You mustn't** smoke there.
Will I be allowed to visit Anne in hospital? — **I don't see why not.**

4. Vorliebe, Abneigung, Gleichgültigkeit (Preferences, Dislikes, Indifference)

a) What can you say if you like something?

I like	books.
	reading detective stories (best).
I prefer	books **to** magazines.
	reading **to** watching TV.
I enjoy	a good football match.
	playing football.
I love	parties/travelling by plane.
It's nice	to get up late.
It's interesting	to watch monkeys

Surfing **is nice/great/wonderful/fantastic.**
My main interest/hobby is collecting stamps.

b) What can you say if you don't like something?

I don't like	cigarettes.
	smoking a pipe.
	smoking **at all.**
I don't enjoy	modern jazz.
	listening to modern jazz.
I hate	onions.
	eating beans.
	eating cabbage **most.**
It's not nice	to get up early.
It's not interesting	to help in the house.

Doing tests **is awful/terrible.**

c) What can you say if you are not really interested in something?

I'm not really interested in games like football or hockey.
I don't mind watching car racing.
Shall we go by train or by bus? — **I don't mind. It's all the same to me.**

5. Pläne (Plans)

What can you say if you want to talk about plans?

What are you doing this evening? — **I'm** meeting some friends.
When are we going to paint the dining-room? — **We could do it** next Saturday.
What are your plans for tomorrow? — **Nothing special.**
What shall we do at the week-end? — **What about** a trip to the Lake District?

Let's hitch to the seaside. — **Can't you think of anything better?**
I know what we can do. We can go swimming. — I can't. I've got a bad cold.
I've got an idea: let's have a barbecue. — **Great.** I hope it won't rain.
Why don't we go to a football match? — **That's a good idea,** if we can still get tickets.

6. Zustimmung und Ablehnung (Agreement, Refusal/Disagreement)

a) What can you say if you want to accept an invitation?

Would you like to go to the pop festival on Saturday?

Oh, yes.
All right.
O.K.
I don't mind.
Oh, great/fine/wonderful.
That's a good idea.
I certainly would.
Of course I would.
I'd love to.

b) What can you say if you want to refuse an invitation?

No, thanks./No, I (certainly) wouldn't.
I'm sorry, I can't.
I'm afraid I can't.
Unfortunately I can't.
I'd love to, but I haven't got time.
I can't. I've got a lot to do.
I don't really want to.
I'm **not** strong **enough** yet after my illness.
But it's **too** expensive.

c) What can you say if you agree with something?

Girls *can't* play football.

That's true.
You're right.
You're quite right.
They certainly can't.
Of course they can't.
I must say they're not very good at it.

d) What can you say if you don't agree?

That's not true./You're not right./You're wrong.
That's not fair./That's unfair.
Rubbish, of course they can.
Don't be silly.
How stupid can you get?
What a silly/stupid thing to say.

7. Überraschung, Freude, Enttäuschung, Ärger, Bedauern
(Surprise, Pleasure, Disappointment, Anger, Regret)

a) What can you say if you feel surprised, happy, disappointed or angry?

Look!
Look at that boy over there.
What a surprise!
Great!/Fantastic!/Fabulous!
How nice/wonderful!
That's lovely/great/etc.
Isn't that lovely/great/etc.
Hasn't she got a pretty hat!
I'm so glad to see you.
We're looking forward to seeing you again next week.
I feel quite happy about that.
Hooray! I've won the first prize.

Oh dear, the bus is full!
Good heavens, the train is gone!
Oh my God, my purse has been stolen!
Oh hell, the damned thing's broken!
What a shock, Colin's broken his leg!
Mrs White's son has been drowned. **How terrible/awful!**
Our team lost 5:0. I'm very **disappointed.**
John didn't tell me the truth. I'm very **angry with him.**
That's not fair.
It's so unfair.
What a lousy trick.

b) What can you say if you feel sorry about something?

I was **sorry** to hear about your accident. — Well, things could be worse.
I'm afraid I can't stay until the end of the film. — Never mind, I'll tell you about it tomorrow.
It's a pity we've missed our bus to the airport. — Don't worry, we can always take a taxi.

8. Möglichkeit, Wahrscheinlichkeit, Sicherheit
(Possibility, Probability, Certainty)

a) What can you say if you think something is possible, probable or certain?

This man **could** be a reporter.
You could be right.
It's possible that I'll go to London next week.
Perhaps Jane will come with me.

We'll **probably** leave on Tuesday.
We'll **most probably** go by train.
I think John's in his bedroom.

I know he's somewhere in the house.
That's true, I saw him 5 minutes ago.
She'll **certainly** send you a postcard.
This **must** be your coat.
I'm sure it's yours.
It's true that he swam across the Thames.
I believe he's a good swimmer.

b) What can you say if you are not sure about something or if you don't believe something?

I'm not sure what time he's coming.
I don't know if you like modern jazz.
I've no idea where my brother is now.
Perhaps he has**n't** got your letter.
They're **probably not** at home.

You **can't** be serious about that.
I don't think he is a reporter.
I don't think you're right.
That **can't be true.**
I don't believe a word of it.

9. Begründungen (Giving Reasons)

What can you say if you want to ask or give the reason for something?

Why are you visiting Germany? — **Because** I want to learn German.
Why hasn't John come with you? — He's ill.
Get the suitcase down, please. — I can't. It's **too** high up.
Push the car into the garage. — I can't. I'm not strong **enough.**
Where are you going? — I forgot a few things, **so** I'm going back to the shop.
Are there any sausages left? — No, we were **so** hungry **that** we ate them all.
Where have you been? — I went to the bank **(in order) to** get some money.